SO FRAIL II

TOXIC FEMININITY

By: Racine McGee

For my mother Diane; the earth from which I originate. I thank you for the life you have given me; which I must give to the world. Through distance and time, our love remains untarnished. For all that you have given me, I thank you and I love you.

Through our differences on my quest to become a man, may my apologies be accepted, my mistakes forgiven and my love, never forgotten.

No need for dissertations; we just need dialogue.

I give these words with the hopes of reaching the sons of my brothers and sisters.

Ubuntu.

Dedicated to Shaquail Anderson and all the brothers whose lives were cut short due to senseless violence.

Asé.

CONTENTS

FEMININITY DEFINED

Before anything is thoroughly expressed, it must be specifically defined. For the context and perspective of this work, femininity will be defined as the spiritual, mental and physical embodiment of the essence of synthesis and construction. Furthermore, unless otherwise specified, any reference to femininity will not be associated with the female gender. Through societal conditioning, femininity has been defaulted to the female gender, exclusively. This notion is limited in scope and serves as the impetus for this writing. Femininity is a point of duality that is manifested in both men and women. As I give my expression, I will speak on femininity as it affects and effects my

1

brothers and me, exclusively. As with my presentation in So Frail: A Reality to Black Male Masculinity, read my words through an objective lens and take nothing personal.

Femininity, as its divine intention, is the polarity that governs the attributes of intuition, emotionality and subjectivity; on its basic level. When harmonized with masculinity, intuition is balanced with and by intelligence; emotionality is balanced with and by rationale; and subjectivity is balanced with and by objectivity. In short, the singularity of life is comprised of the polarity between principles (masculinity) and details (femininity). The details allude to what is felt and the principles allude to what is thought. With the comprehension of this balance, it can be understood why femininity is predisposed, but not exclusive, to the female gender and masculinity is predisposed, not exclusive, to the male gender. Women feel and men think, naturally. As previously stated, only when specified will there be an association with the gender. That previous statement, and the statement to follow, will be the few instances in which that association is made.

In modern times, my brothers and I have not been embodying our natural predisposition of masculinity. For quite some time, we have been feminine men. Now, if your immediate thought following that sentence made you feel as if I am calling my brothers soft and/or homosexual, you are substantiating the point. You are subjectively responding (femininity) to an objectively expressed idea (masculinity). Furthermore, you have relegated the conceptualizations of masculinity and femininity to their basic, carnal manifestations.

A feminine man is one who operates through the spiritual, mental and physical embodiment of the essence of synthesis and construction. Therefore, one can be a "manly" man and still operate through femininity. In all actuality, that is the current dynamic for the vast majority of us. Our polarity has been directed to synthesis and construction. Not that we cannot synthesize and construct, but we do so devoid of analyzing and deconstructing; which is our natural predisposition. By utilizing the polarity we are misinterpreting over the predisposed polarity that has been stripped away from us, we are not achieving our highest essence as Black men; which was spoken on in more detail in So Frail.

As I mentioned in So Frail, this is NOT a means to attack, demean, demoralize or degrade any of my brothers. I have nothing but love for us all. However, with that love comes correction. Our current stance as men has become very destructive to ourselves, our women, our children and our communities. This must be changed and permanently evolved in order for us to move forward and bring about the necessary peace that our people need. In order to do this, we must thoroughly understand what we have become since our divine masculinity was stripped away from us. Not only did we become feminine men, we became toxic feminine men; and when creative energy is poisoned with toxicity, destruction will be the only outcome.

TOXIC FEMININITY

Within all things exists a polarity to
balance it. For life, there is death. For joy,
there is pain. For love, there is hate. For
peace, there is chaos. For femininity, there is
masculinity. Moreover, within all single
things there exists a dual nature, or antithesis
if you will. This dual nature can be better
understood as a "shadow side." This is the
aspect of the thing that carries every attribute
in the exact capacity but it has a completely
opposite outcome in its manifestation; sort of
like an evil twin. Nothing can escape this dual
nature. For life, there can be one of peace or
one of turmoil; death can be peaceful or
tragic. Just as masculinity can be frail or

fortified, femininity can be healthy or toxic; and toxic femininity will be the singularity of this discussion. Remember, femininity is defined as the spiritual, mental and physical embodiment of the essence of synthesis and construction. This work is speaking on its polarity and not a gender association.

When it comes to femininity, the polarity governs synthesis and construction. Therefore, the nature of femininity is creation. To take it one step further, the outcome if its manifestation would be to build or destroy. So, when it comes to femininity there can be the healthy expression, which builds, or the toxic expression, which destroys. There is often misinterpretation when viewing masculinity and toxic femininity through the means which I define them. One will ask, "What's the difference if masculinity governs analysis and deconstruction and toxic femininity is about destruction?" The answer resides in the two words destruction and deconstruction.

Although the two words are close in spelling and sometimes used as synonyms, they are not defined the same. To deconstruct something means to dissect it into its individual parts. By separating it into its individual parts, it can be reconstituted into its whole. To destroy something means to completely obliterate it. Once something is destroyed, it can never be restored to its original state. This reveals that masculinity is the polarity that balances with femininity and toxic femininity is the shadow side to the outcome of femininity's manifestation. This manifestation is what has been infused in and dominates the psyches of my brothers; relentlessly for centuries.

It has been previously argued that our masculinity is frail and fragile. The truth is that it is neither. In reality, it is absent and has been replaced with femininity. Yes, we have been operating as feminine men. Once again, if your mind immediately went to me calling us sweet, soft or homosexual, you substantiate the idea. Masculinity is a polarity that respects objectivity and rationale. It sees what is being spoken, as it is spoken. Femininity respects subjectivity and emotion. It sees beyond what is being spoken as it understands its associations. To reaffirm a previous point, masculinity acknowledges the principles and femininity acknowledges the details. When acknowledging details through a toxic lens, you get toxic femininity; or pseudo-masculinity, as expressed in So Frail.

Our operation through toxic femininity comes from subconsciously understanding that we are to balance with the feminine component while consciously misinterpreting our masculine component. The subconscious mind respects the polarities of masculinity and femininity. It understands that the aspects reside in us both; with

9

femininity predisposed to women and masculinity predisposed to men. However, the conscious mind is purposely tainted to create an imbalance between the polarities by establishing disharmony between the wielders of the predispositions. This is accomplished by shutting down masculinity and promoting toxic femininity through a falsified perception that encourages and strengthens its existence.

There are many principles to femininity. For the sake of my writings, I use intuition, emotionality and subjectivity. These three principles serve as the strongest to express the notions of synthesis and construction. I won't go too far back into history as current circumstances are enough to express the emergence of toxic femininity and the manipulation of masculinity through these points alone. Remember, toxic femininity is the shadow side to healthy femininity. This would then transform intuition into insecurity; forces the expression of negative emotions over positive ones; and leads to the negative details of subjectivity being expressed over the positive ones. As I express these points, I will elaborate on how the masculine component is manipulated and the feminine component is strengthened and made toxic. I will begin with intuition.

Intuition is the ability to reconstitute information that has been deconstructed via intelligence. This reconstitution follows the characteristics defined within femininity as the spiritual, mental and physical embodiment of the essence of synthesis and construction. What this signifies is that intuition is a means to apply the information obtained through intelligence, transform it through wisdom and elevate it through understanding. Without the balancing component of intelligence, no being's intuition will ever reach its pinnacle. Well, at least not the healthy pinnacle that it should embody.

When there is no intelligence to balance with and strengthen itself, intuition remains dormant. Even deeper, when that masculine component is forced into its shadow side, it caters to the emergence of the toxic form of intuition; which is insecurity. The shadow side of intelligence is ignorance. As intelligence is the obtaining of knowledge and information, ignorance is the abstaining from those. In today's society, there is a common cliché that ignorance is bliss. The acceptance of this mantra opens the door for a dangerous mentality. When it comes to me and my brothers, this mentality has effects that have paved the way for generations of calamity; completely poisoning our intuitive nature.

It is no mystery that there is a school to prison pipeline. We speak about it daily. Yet, we rarely dissect its direct effects and impositions on Black male masculinity. According to various resources, third grade test scores are used to build prisons. Black men are among the majority of the prison population. Through basic critical thinking, it stands to reason that the miseducation from kindergarten to third grade, generally ages 5 to 9, is significant enough to guarantee a seat in a prison cell. Let that marinate for a second before I show how this ties in. A criminal is created in school between the ages of 5 to 9, just waiting to commit their first crime. SMH.

The purpose of education is to promote intelligence. However, the current education system does not promote intelligence. Rather, it promotes and relishes the idea of rote memorization. If you are unfamiliar with that idea, rote memorization is simply regurgitating information under the guise that one is learning. In fact, you do not learn at all; instead you develop a great memory. This is why schools tend to promote spelling and trivia competitions for the entire school while there are only clubs for science and math. Spelling and trivia require memorization of details (feminine component) while science and math require the understanding of principles (masculine component). Here is why this is important. If the student does not understand the principles of the subject, the changing details will always confuse them. When a student remains confused by the details as they are moved to more challenging principles, it's a matter of time before they give up.

Now, let's tie this back into the school to prison pipeline. If prisons are built according to third grade test scores, it is obvious that it is known that these children are not understanding what they are learning. Therefore, a criminal is not innately born, they are created in the school system. Furthermore, as it relates to this writing, their intelligence is neither nurtured nor promoted. When intelligence is reduced, ignorance is enhanced. As previously stated, intelligence is a masculine attribute through its ability to analyze and deconstruct information. Therefore, the shadow side of intelligence, ignorance, is the inability to analyze and deconstruct information. When this shadow side of the masculine component balances with its feminine polarity, the feminine side becomes toxic. This means that when ignorance meets intuition, intuition becomes insecurity; its shadow side.

Before I go too much further, understand that I am not calling myself or my brothers criminals. What I am expressing is how toxic femininity is created through the manipulation of the masculine polarity. This manipulation ultimately leads to the manifestations that can lead to a criminal mind; simply because the feminine polarity governs synthesis and construction. Hence why when femininity is shifted to the point of toxicity, destruction will follow. Taking it one step deeper, I used that concept to expound upon how the school to prison pipeline plays the greatest role in our expression of toxic femininity by manipulating masculinity through the suppression of intelligence. Trust me, the system is not failing. It is working exactly as it should. But I digress.

Another pivotal point to femininity is emotionality. Emotions are feminine in essence because they enhance the things in which they are connected to. Basically, they fuel the details added to the principles. In modern times, femininity is relegated to its carnal understanding of gender. This leads to the falsified idea that being emotional is a sign that a man is conducting himself as a woman. If we remain on the carnal frequencies of life, this is a true statement. However, when we understand this from its truest expression, it's a stupid idea. Emotions are the feminine, operative force necessary to balance a being with its masculine, rational nature. Just as the masculine component of intelligence must harmonize with the feminine component of intuition, so too does emotionality balance with rationale. If you are familiar with So Frail, I spoke about what gang life is at its core. It's the fusion of barbarism and self-hatred. Although both are toxic energies, barbarism will be the focus as it pertains to toxic femininity. But before I express that, I must explain it from the masculine side first.

Rationale is the ability to view circumstances in the presence of emotions without being affected or effected by them. Understand that a rational being does not omit emotions. Rather, emotions are unable to dictate the thought process and actions of the rational being. On the coin flip to that, the shadow side of rationale is irrationality. To be irrational is to lose the ability to prevent emotions from dictating ones thoughts and actions. This now connects to barbarism because there is no logic to the barbaric nature. The only objective is to kill and obliterate. Period. I tend to view barbarism as killing everything and feeling nothing. Now, don't misunderstand what I am saying. All fighting is not irrational behavior. However, that distinction is made very clear between the ideas of warriors and barbarians. Warriors think before they fight. Barbarians fight before they think. As of current times, we have been operating through the barbaric nature.

At this moment, accountability and responsibility must be taken by the Civil Rights movement. In their quest to integrate and become equal with barbaric beings, they achieved the goal; just not as they thought they were achieving it. What came from that movement was the assimilation into a barbaric culture. As if self-hatred wasn't high enough prior to the movement, it significantly increased once the "integration" was signed into congress. This was the first major mark of the transformation of the masculine component into its shadow side.

Understand that I respect the movement for what it tried to do; but the respect stops there. Not for the people, for the movement. There is no rationale in seeking equality and morality from a being who has actively shown me that they do not value or respect my existence. If I become equal to that, what does that do to me? It makes me a being who does not value or respect his own existence. There is absolutely no rationale in that. But, I digress.

Following the Civil Rights movement, we assimilated into a barbaric culture. One of the major tenets of this culture is the idea that "men don't cry." This assertion is the main impetus for how the feminine component of emotionality is made toxic. On a deeper level of understanding, tears are the physical manifestations of a soul's release of something. Although commonly associated with "bad manifestations," tears range from joy to sorrow as the soul is releasing the energy associated with that particular emotion. Tears of joy, tears from laughter, tears of happiness; all a release of the energy felt within the soul. And those are positive emotions; ones we should feel as men. Yet, when tears begin to form, we immediately stop them by suppressing, and repressing, emotions. Why? Simply because we've been conditioned not to cry instead of being taught to understand what we are crying for. Basically, the ability to rationalize emotions. What we have learned to do is irrationalize our emotions. This has forced us to internalize them rather than release them. So when the shadow side of rationale meets emotionality, a fuse is lit. A very short fuse that will be responsible for the toxic expression of emotionality.

Toxic femininity is dangerous in its own right. When it comes to the component of emotionality, it is completely destr

because only three emotions ever res

this harmony of irrationality and em

Those emotions are anger, rage and/or

aggression. When you've internalized

everything you've ever experienced since a

child, you contain more volatility than a

shaken soda bottle. It's really just a matter of

time before you explode.

Through the medium in which we've

been conditioned, our masculinity has been

erroneously defined through the lens of toxic

femininity. As it relates to the component of

rationale, this leads us to submerge ourselves

in the I Don't Give a Fuck, Fuck Everybody

and Never Scared attitudes we embody.

Couple these attitudes from the shadow side

of rationale with the anger, rage and

aggression that stems from the toxicity of

emotionality and you get a Real Nigga. A

manifestation heavily promoted in our

communities that can only lead to destruction.

Now, I get that we "mean" a real man, strong man, confident man, etc. when we use it. But a 6 years old child singing to his favorite trap song about a Real Nigga "fuckin' bitches, gettin' money, killin' niggas, runnin' trains on hoes, hatin' niggas," etc., is writing these mantras into his mind every time that song plays. He does not see the effects as his parents bounce to it and turn up with it playing as a good time is happening. The child's mind has made the association that the manifestation of a real nigga is a good thing. But if we peel back the layers, a real nigga is a being operating through a barbaric nature with a mentality of self-hatred. In war with barbaric people, the barbarians desecrate the land, kill all the men and children, rape the women and keep the riches of the land as booty; or spoils of war. Go up a few lines and reread the part about "a 6 years old child singing…" and see the similarities. While you do that, I'll move on to the final point of subjectivity so we can close this out.

Subjectivity is the manner in which a thing is perceived by the observer. It is a feminine component because subjectivity receives its credence through synthesis and construction. The observer sees a thing and the mind creates the reality based on details found within perception and prior experiences. For example, if I describe a black dog with brown paws, brown around the mouth and a snipped tail, one person may visualize a Dobermann Pinscher and another may picture a Rottweiler. Although they share the same description (principle), the specific details are different. A Dobermann is generally lean and tall while a Rottweiler is shorter and chubby. This is how subjectivity works. Subjectivity is the fuel by which the details are used to describe an object.

With subjectivity as a feminine polarity, its balancing, masculine polarity is objectivity. Objectivity is the ability to see something as it is. Nothing more, nothing less. To revisit the dog example, objectivity will not see a Dobermann or a Rottweiler. It will see a black dog with brown paws, brown around the mouth and a snipped tail. The reason for this is because objectivity is fueled by the principles used to define an object in the same fashion that subjectivity is fueled by the details used to describe an object.

To expound upon how objectivity is suppressed, we must revisit two points. One point being that the female gender has the predisposition for femininity. The other point being the school to prison pipeline. I spoke about the pipeline being potent enough to diminish intelligence between ages 5 to 9. During this same time frame, and beyond, it also aides in diminishing objectivity by way of being taught by female teachers in a structure that promotes rote memorization. What this means is that a Black male, with a predisposition for the masculine polarity, is being taught by a female teacher, with the predisposition for the feminine polarity, how to memorize details; as opposed to solidifying principles. This is NOT to say that we cannot be taught by women. This is saying that women naturally see the details before seeing principles and men see principles before seeing details. Therefore, in a class where women are teaching children through the lens of details, how to learn through details, the child who is predisposed to learn through principles will struggle. [This is heavily evident in our relationships. Women will send a lengthy text message almost 4 pages long; only to get upset when we respond to the end or a few points. We extracted the principles out of all the details you sent and responded with the principle. This is why we ask "Why you trippin'?" when you tell us to have a good life after we just responded to your rant.] Those who struggle tend to fall behind, then eventually drop out. Those who succeed are shifted to lead with their feminine polarity. Because there are two paths which emerge from this battle against masculinity, there are two dynamics to this expression of toxic femininity. One being the emotionally unavailable (EU) path where the principles and objectivity were maintained and the other being the catty, argumentative (CA) path where the details and subjectivity are pushed forward.

As it pertains to the EU path, the unavailability is due to the absence and/or suppression of the masculine essence with the rejection of the feminine essence. As previously defined, masculinity is the spiritual, mental, and physical embodiment of the essence of analysis and deconstruction. As it relates here, the specific component to that is objectivity. In order to thoroughly comprehend details, one must be able to objectify them. It must be understood why a detail is decorating a principle in order to comprehend it and engage in a healthy experience. This is highly evident in regards to our emotions. My brothers and I are taught, encouraged and conditioned to avoid all emotions we may feel because they are said to make us soft or weak if we embrace them. What this leads to is our inability to deal with them internally. In turn, it leads to our inability to deal with them externally. This inability is the direct cause for a nonchalant "Oh word? That's crazy," response in our relationships. It's not that we do not care. We do not know how to care appropriately about the situation because we have not developed an objective approach to balance with subjective experiences. Thus, the expression of being emotionally unavailable through our lack of objectivity.

The second dynamic is the CA path. This path is caused by the absence and/or suppression of the masculine essence while embracing the feminine essence. The key point still resides in the lack of the objective position required to balance subjective impositions. This causes us to see the details as something more than they are. Let's refer to the dog example previously discussed; taking it one step further. A black dog with brown paws, brown around the mouth and a snipped tail could be a Dobermann or a Rottweiler if the subjectivity is healthy. However, when it is toxic, this leads to that dog being a Dobermann, a Rottweiler, a Pitt Bull with a brown mother and black father, a chocolate lab and a golden retriever mix or several other amalgamations of dog breeds. This is the toxic expression, in its simplest dynamic, because the objectivity never enters to limit the description to the two logical possibilities. These expressions of toxic femininity are better understood with our relationships with women; the beings naturally predisposed to femininity.

The EU path leads us to be dismissive to emotions because our objective nature won't allow us to see the emotion as a thing. It causes us to have difficulty seeing the principle of the expressed emotion. Because we cannot see the principle, this forces us to reject what is being presented to us. This particular path is captured in mantras like "I don't love that bitch." "I don't love..." is the rejection of the feminine essence of emotion. "...that bitch." is caused by the shadow side to the masculine expression of objectivity. The object (as in topic of discussion), a woman, is viewed negatively as a bitch. To embrace this ideology of not loving a bitch strengthens the emotional unavailability of the man. So when we say, with conviction, things like "fuck these bitches," "these hoes ain't shit," etc. we further tap into the toxic feminine energy of the emotionally unavailable manifestation. On the other side of that, the CA path leads to being defensive

29

towards emotions by embracing the subjectivity without objectivity's expression. This causes us to see far more than what is being expressed. The greatest example of this is when we feel we are being nagged. We FEEL this way because we do not objectively accept the subject that is presented to us. We take it as an attack; forcing us to retaliate. We see this as an attack because we see more than what is being expressed. For example, I witnessed a mother tell her son to go do something productive with his son because it was snowing outside. The son flipped on his mother saying that he takes care of his son, he always does productive things with his son, he is not a bad father, etc. None of that was ever stated by his mother. However toxic femininity through its CA manifestation forced him to see details that were not there because his objective essence could not limit the internalization of his mother's words solely to what she said. Rather, it caused him to see far more than she had spoken. Which led to his completely unnecessary retaliation and verbal onslaught towards his mother. How many of us have responded to women this way before? Admit it and accept it so we can heal and move forward.

Toxic femininity is what we are currently operating under as Black men. This polarity has been conditioned and perpetually reconditioned within our minds. Although it has become a normalcy, it is not normal. It is a poison to our existence and everyday way of life. Yes, as beings we have the feminine essence within us. However, it should not be expressed through its toxic form. It should be presented through its healthy form in harmony with our truer masculine nature. As long as we continue to operate through toxic femininity, our masculinity will remain frail and we will be of absolutely no service to our people. In order to begin this healing, transformation and restoration process, we must address our relationships with our fathers. Those who were absent and those who were present. Both play a major part in the infusion of the toxic femininity within our psyches.

DADDY'S MAYBE: INITIAL EFFEMINIZATION

The most important piece to the manifestation of toxic femininity is directly related to our relationships with our fathers. If it is understood how the manifestations of toxic femininity can either lead to the EU man or the CA man, the observations to be explained will also be understood. Before I begin, I will say what I'm already sure will be spoken; some, not all. I'm well aware that it is not all of us. If it doesn't apply, let it fly. However, it is quite enough to make an observation that can be substantiated worlds over. We must thoroughly comprehend that the majority is enough to influence the minority. If we are practicing "every man for himself" over Ubuntu, we are merely delaying the inevitable destruction. We must operate as the collective, not as the individual. If my toxic feminine son meets the daughter of a "some, not all," an entire nation has been destroyed before it was ever created. So it is imperative that we tackle this together without using mentalities imposed upon us through assimilation and integration. A victory in a battle means nothing when the war was lost. Never forget that.

When it comes to our influence in our sons lives, we must acknowledge both absent and present fathers. We must not assume we are absolved from this because we are in our sons' lives. With all due respect to my brothers, you do not get an A simply because you put your name on the paper to acknowledge the assignment is yours. In some classes, attendance is 10% of the final grade. Keeping with this metaphor, showing up and doing nothing else/bare minimum means you still fail the class. So understand that this is not simply to speak on absent fathers. No leaf will be left unturned and all will be discussed. As I stated before, I love all my brothers. But with love comes correction. Therefore, we must be willing to address all that goes into us; and more.

By now, we are familiar with the two manifestations of toxic femininity. The EU and the CA. If these paths are evident in our methods, they don't suddenly vanish when we become fathers. If we have not acknowledged fatherhood through the scope of toxic femininity we will continue the cycle; passing the behavior on to our sons. Whether absent or present, we will create the template that our sons will emulate in the future. It is said that a child's personality is developed by the time they are 6 years old. This is when we, as fathers, must be the most proactive so we are not reactive down the line. Although it's a harsh reality to face, we must accept that we are the direct cause for the continuation of the effeminization of our sons. We, and we alone, have the power to end it. There is no greater influence over our boys than us. If we are planting these seeds, we must see to it that the fruit both thrives and multiplies into its healthiest expression.

When it comes to fatherhood, absent fathers remain on the chopping block; with just reason. They will not receive a pass here either. However, it must be noted that sometimes a present father can infuse just as much, if not more, poison into his children than an absent father. You can be there and not be there. But remember, this is not an opportunity to attack my brothers. This is a means to shed light on a dynamic that may or may not be identifiable to us all.

When a present father raises a child through the filter of toxic femininity, he is setting a standard that will be codified by the

dynamics of being EU, CA or an
amalgamation of both positions. Through the
former dynamic, a father sets an example for
his son to become an emotionless being. The
EU father has the biggest influence on
stripping his son of his smile and solidifying
the stigma that boys do not cry. A smile is
generally the physical manifestation of joyous
emotions such as excitement, happiness and
elation. A son learns to express these
emotions through his interaction with his
father. It is strengthened when his father hugs
him, holds him, kisses him and expresses his
love for him. It is not homosexual or
pedophilic to engage in these activities with
your son. It becomes homosexual and
pedophilic when it is made into sexual
activities with your son. Intention precedes
thought and thought precedes action. If your
intentions and thoughts are in that space, your
actions then become perverse. If what I
expressed immediately led you to think about

homosexuality or pedophilia, you are beginning to see how toxic femininity fuels our essence over masculinity. Subjectivity took you to a place that objectivity had no intention of going. But, I digress.

As fathers, it is imperative that we show love and appreciation to our sons. It will not make them, or you, soft or weak. In fact, it will make them significantly stronger. The only thing more powerful than someone willing to die for something is someone willing to live for it. If there is no love, there is no life. A son with no life inside of him has difficulty accepting that it is okay to smile; simply because a smile is the response to emotions that many sons never had a chance to experience from their fathers. Ask a brother why he mean mugs and his response will fall into the parameters of there being no reason to smile. At the core, that means having no emotions to trigger that physical manifestation. Smile my brothers. It's okay.

We must stop creating sons who are afraid to and cannot feel. Feeling is okay.

It's also okay to cry. Crying is another aspect that the EU father will prevent his son from doing. Crying is not a disease or a mutation we should be afraid of. This is also not to say that we should boo-hoo cry every chance we get. Crying is a release of the burdens bound to the soul. Rather than teaching our sons not to cry, we should be teaching them to understand why they are crying and express that burden. If you ask a young boy why he is crying, his initial response is to try to stop crying immediately instead of telling you what he is crying for. Why? Because he believes he is acting like a punk or a little girl. Being upset makes him a punk. Being disappointed makes him a punk. Being sad makes him a punk. Why? Because each of those emotions trigger the tears that will release the burden from his soul. However, he cannot release this burden for the fear of being a punk in his father's eyes. This runs deeper because if a father is encouraging his son to be greater than him, this will lead to a son who out does his father in his emotional unavailability. To my brothers, we must break this emotionless mentality. We are doing nothing but creating heartless sons and this cannot go on any further. We must break this cycle and mode of thought immediately. However, we must insure that we are doing it from the healthy expression. Otherwise, we will be fueling it through the other manifestation of being CA.

The present CA father will set an example for his son to be volatile and disrespectful as an expression of being a man. This manifestation of toxic femininity is the most detrimental form. It's what leads us to be physically, mentally and spiritually abusive towards ourselves, our women, our children and our people. Words are the most powerful entities in our lives. I call words entities because they carry energies that, when spoken, can change an entire reality once the words are released. A father expressing the CA form of toxic femininity will teach his son how to destroy life in all that he comes across without the slightest ounce of remorse.

A son first learns how he should engage with people by how he sees his father engage with people. Children are unbiased in their development and easily see things as they are. For a child, the behavior they accept is not based on right or wrong. Instead, it is based on habit and normalcy. If I see my father impulsively explode when someone disagrees with him, I will impulsively explode when someone disagrees with me. If I see my father yell to be heard, I will yell to be heard. If I witness my father abuse my mother when he is angry, I will abuse my mother/women when I'm angry. I will not see it as right or wrong but as a normalcy through my upbringing. An upbringing established through toxic femininity that creates my volatile and disrespectful nature.

This nature creates a façade that is deemed manliness when we say what we feel. The poison to this is that we only feel negative emotions of rage, anger and aggression. Therefore, the words fueled through these energies can only destroy. What this does to our sons is plants a seed of destruction that we nurture. In our friendships with our brothers, our sons witness us smile and befriend people we speak negatively towards. What's more is that we use the same form of speech in good and bad times. For example, one friend can be roasting us and we'll chuckle and say, "Man, fuck you." That same friend can say something that pinches a nerve and we say, "Man, fuck you." Same exact words but totally different energy behind them. But remember, children don't accept behavior based on what is right or wrong. They accept it based on habit and normalcy. If my father befriends someone who he says, "fuck you" to in various connotations, I too will have friendships just like that.

This entire concept was beautifully captured in the movie Menace II Society. In the opening scene, Caine's father is playing cards at the table with a group of friends. He asks one of his friends for the money he owes him. Just to paraphrase, the friend says, "Man, fuck you. I'll pay you when I feel like it." The other friends at the table laugh after he says this. It is important to note that they laughed because it's revealing that this is normal behavior. We laugh when friends bump heads like this because it's a normalcy and things typically don't go sour. But in this instance, Caine's father pulls a gun out and shoots the friend. Caine wakes up before the shots are fired and sees his father kill a man. Of course, this sticks to Caine's subconscious mind.

Fast forward to a point in the movie where Caine gets shot in the shoulder. Once he is released from the hospital, he meets up with his best friend O-Dog and they talk about the shooting. Paraphrasing again, O-Dog tells Caine "You were cryin' like a little bitch" and Caine laughs and responds with, "Fuck you. That shit hurt." It was such a lighthearted expression despite the choice of words. But this reveals what influences are given to the son. His friendships were patterned by his father's. Now, let's fast forward just a bit further.

The next scene of discussion involves Caine and his friends at Caine's girlfriend's house. At the beginning of the scene, Caine's friend Chauncey is trying to flirt with Caine's girlfriend. Caine laughs and says, "Chill Chauncey." Chauncey responds with, "You know I'm joking. You my nigga Caine." It's left alone and Caine and his friends go to play cards. Chauncey attempts to flirt with Caine's girlfriend a second time and goes too far. Caine asks O-Dog for his gun then pistol whips Chauncey. As they pull Caine off of Chauncey, you can hear him say, "Man, fuck you." Same thing he said to O-Dog with a very different connotation.

Please don't get me wrong here. Chauncey deserved what he got. He should have left her alone; cause and effect took its natural course. The purpose of this was to illustrate how the CA expression of toxic femininity is cyclic from father to son; to show how this manifestation has created a normalcy of volatility and disrespect. Caine's father was volatile because his friend disrespected him. Caine became volatile because Chauncey disrespected him. All four of these men were operating through the medium of toxic femininity and destruction manifested into their realities.

Granted, this is a major extreme and it can be diluted to smaller scaled circumstances. I used this, along with the perspective of the EU father, to show that toxic femininity, in real time, is an amalgamation of these two extremes. When a father passes this on to his son, his son develops the barbaric nature I spoke on earlier. One where the mentality is to kill everything (CA) and feel nothing (EU). This is why I mentioned that the present father does not get a pass simply because he is in his son's life. You can be there and not be there at all; and what you are there for can have nothing of substance for your son. With that said, we shall continue on to the absent father who is fueled through this manifestation.

The absent father expressing toxic femininity is the indirect cause of the emasculation of his son by being the direct cause of the effeminization of his son. The absent EU father will leave his son with more questions than answers. The absent CA father will leave his son with more answers than questions. In either outcome, the son is left to fend for himself.

Now, the question is how does the absent father play a part in his son's development if he isn't there? This is answered by a concept called genetic memory. I won't go heavy into the details as this writing does not call for that depth of information. However, genetic memory is what is passed on through conception. On the basic level, there are genotypes and phenotypes. I like to view phenotypes as the tangible/physical aspects and the genotypes as the intangible/mental aspects. The phenotype is what would give me my father's eyes and nose. The genotype is what would give me my father's mentality and thought process. For the sake of this writing, I will use the genotype as the phenotype is pretty obvious.

The genotype is the intangible aspect inherited by the child. More so, this inheritance is the result of the DNA's expression at the moment of conception. The thoughts, feelings and emotions during copulation are stored in and transferred from the DNA of the parents to the child. If the child is conceived through "makeup" sex, those genetic memories are passed to the child. If the child is conceived as a reconciliation for infidelity, those genetic memories will be passed to the child. If the child is conceived in a moment of disconnection and/or opposition, those genetic memories are passed to the child. This is why during slavery the premise was to break the mind and build the body. The body was the phenotypic expression of the genetics and the mind was the genotypic expression. A child born of physically strong but mentally weak parents becomes easier to enslave because their DNA is carrying the genetic memory of the already enslaved parents. But, I digress.

So the purpose of parenting, from the universal/cosmological level, is to teach your children how to unlock the aspects of you that are found within their DNA and genetic memory banks. As it pertains to this writing, the absent father is not available to help his son "unlock his father within himself." This is how and why a son born of an absent EU father has more questions than answers and the son born of an absent CA father has more answers than questions. The manner in which their genetic memories are unlocked are understood differently.

The absent EU father is the father who is completely absent. He has nothing to do with his son; good, bad or indifferent. A son born to this father will unlock and understand the characteristics of his genetic memory through trial and error and self-actualization. This type of son is often mistaken for being stubborn and prideful. This misunderstanding is far from the truth. The reasoning behind him isolating and becoming independent and self-reliant is because things are releasing within him that do not resonate with any familiarity from his environment. It's not that he does not want help or is unwilling to ask for it. However, what he is feeling within himself is something that only his father can help him understand. This is why there are things a son can only learn from a man; and things he can only learn from his biological father. This is one of the major reasons a son born to an EU father matures into a man who is perceived to need no one. The most difficult challenges of his life came from his understanding of the genetic memory passed to him from a father who didn't help him unlock these things. This, in essence, is a son who "fathered" himself. And if I am my own father, issues pertaining to masculinity and male circumstances are things I will not look outside myself for because I've solved them for myself my entire life.

This is the reason the son born of the absent EU father has more questions than answers. He continually explores himself and finds things he has difficulty understanding. Many of these things create questions that he may never get an answer to because his father is not present to answer those specific father-son questions.

On the opposite side to that, the absent CA father is partially absent. Partially absent because his time away is beyond significant enough to qualify as absent; yet, he periodically returns for confrontation and temporary disruption. Basically, the in and out father who is more out than in. This type of father creates the son who seeks his validation through cliques, gangs, organizations, sets, etc. He receives his self-understanding from Big Homies and OG's because the things that surface within him, he knows that a father figure should teach him. He does not seek them from his father because of the sporadic and inconsistent relationship he has with him. His method of development is to receive guidance outside of himself. This is why this type of son has more answers than questions. It's problematic, however, because his answers are coming from multiple sources at any given time. This provides a level of insecurity that creates an illusory version of himself. A version that keeps him from being who he truly is; while still drawing on his essence.

For example, a son can have an innate affinity for chemistry. He can easily balance chemical equations and understand how molecules can be manipulated to change one substance to another. In his attempt to understand why he has this affinity, he crosses paths with an OG who shows him how to turn cocaine into crack. As "negative" as the details are, the principles are still chemistry to the core. A semi-solid substance is being transformed into a solid substance with significantly more potency. The son enjoys cooking crack. Not because its crack but because of his affinity to the science of chemistry. It just so happens that a drug dealer tapped into that part of him before a chemist ever could. That part of him, however, was only open for exploitation because his CA father was absent; predisposing his son to seek validation from those outside of himself.

So where the son of the absent EU father becomes one who is disconnected from everything outside of himself and self-reliant, the son of the absent CA father becomes one who is attached to multiple things outside of himself and codependent. The former has a strong sense of self; yet, he is rigid in ideology. The latter is fluid in ideology with an insecure sense of self. Both, however, are the results of a father's absence. Whether absent or present, a father will always serve as the template for his son.

This template is the impetus that leads to the effeminization of ourselves and our sons. We must remember that what I am expressing is well above the carnal scope of gender. An effeminized man is not one who simply expresses the tendencies of a woman. It is a man who first loses his essence of analysis and deconstruction (masculinity) to embody synthesis and construction (femininity). As he embodies femininity, his expression is made toxic through several mediums of indoctrination; from assimilation to entertainment. This indoctrination forces his femininity into its shadow side which results in destruction and desecration. This mentality and expression is passed on to the son because it is accepted by the father. It is accepted by the father because it receives respect from the world that is indoctrinating him. The greatest power to ever fuel a man has been, and will always be, respect.

RESPECT

Respect is to men, what love is to women. The extent a woman is willing to go to be loved is just as far as man is willing to go to be respected. From killing his own image to entertaining the masses in a dress, a man's respect can, and in many regards will, supersede his own morals, integrity and rationale. When a man's respect is granted to him through this manifestation of toxic femininity, the more respect he obtains, the more destructive he becomes.

Before I go further, let me first define respect as it pertains to the context of this writing. Respect is a feeling or understanding that someone or something is important and

55

should be treated in an appropriate way. Notice how the definition ends: "...treated in an appropriate way." Period. The entire definition does not allude to respect being granted for any specific behavior, deed or affiliation. Therefore, this definition trumps the ideology that "respect is not given, it is earned." However, we are part of a societal structure where respect isn't defaulted and must be obtained. When we are seeking respect through a skewed vision of toxic femininity, what motives and actions will we exhibit as a means of obtaining this respect? That will be answered along the way. Follow me as we go forward.

In the intro to the song Money, Power & Respect by The Lox, Lil' Kim says, "See, I believe in money, power and respect. First you get the money, then you get the power. After you get the power, mutha fuckahs will respect you." This song came out in 1998. Understand that I am not saying the intro to this song is the cause of what I will be presenting. I am saying that art imitates reality. Therefore, the reality must precede the art to have any relevance to the culture. Furthermore, there is a saying that says the first generation fights the war so the second generation can be educated for the third generation to create the art. What this means is that artistic expression is the manifestation of a generation who fought for their own understanding. Connecting that with the songs intro, we see that the conceptualization of what is needed to get respect (money and power) is the result of the fight required to comprehend respect. Yet, and still, there is more to this puzzle.

When we add the component of the Civil Rights movement and integration, we understand that we fought for equality. But more than equality, we fought to be respected by beings that hated us, viewed us as 3/5 of a human being and only acknowledged us for purposes of entertainment, physical prowess and carnality. As previously stated, integration was truly assimilation into a barbaric culture that thrives on toxic femininity. When we put all of these pieces together, the respect we must "earn" is solidified by our success being substantiated by the standard of our defined enemies in this present circumstance. Solid masculinity will see the insanity in this. However, toxic femininity perceives this destructive ideology as a win. This sets the tone for the "respected" to view themselves as an exception to the atrocities affecting the demographic that looks just like them. But I don't want to deviate from the topic at hand so allow me to continue.

When it comes to respect as viewed by the societal lens, it must be earned. When we go back to the definition I used, a key word of major significance is important. So let's bring this together. My importance as a man is something I must earn. Which means, until I can earn that, I am unimportant. This is not semantics. This is a basic premise of critical thought. Until I have obtained something deemed valuable by the masses, I do not deserve to be respected. Very poisonous ideology; hence how it is infused into toxic femininity. When the respected images that look like me are athletes, entertainers, drug dealers, gangsters and goons, how do you think I am going to "earn" my respect?

Before I answer that, I am going to express an idea that probably crossed a few minds. "Well, you can go to school and become a doctor/lawyer and get respect as well. Those aren't always the only mediums to earn respect as Black men and we should stop thinking that." Very well played. To an extent, I agree. Although you played the ace of spades, the big joker is still in play. Yes, those "professions" do acquire respect for Black men. However, before a Black man is a

Black man, he is a Black boy. We cannot skip over this very important detail. To become a "professional," one must embody discipline, intelligence and dedication. The discipline and dedication, not a problem. The intelligence, on the other hand, not so much.

Contrary to there being an abundant amount of respect for the intelligent Black man, that same respect is marginal for the intelligent Black boy. Before you say, "that's not true," I am not speaking directly on your son. I am speaking collectively on our sons. You may see that your son has the potential to go places; but how many of his best friends do you not want him around because they have "nothing going for them" or you can "see where they will end up?" Be honest here and remember that birds of a feather flock together. Either your son has nothing going for himself or his friends have the same potential to go as far as he can. They aren't friends for nothing. But the perspective is all based on how the Black boy is respected in conjunction with the ideology that respect is not given, it is earned. This ideology is thoroughly understood by our Black sons and they adjust immediately. This adjustment is rooted in doing whatever will grant them respect as they are, not what they can become. Now let's unravel this quilt from beginning to end.

I previously mentioned the school system and the suppression of masculinity through the structured school to prison pipeline. This dynamic was how the adults attack our boys. Now we will uncover how their peers attack them for 13 years. Suppressing masculinity and creating the template that leads a Black boy away from being respected for his intelligence and into the path of being respected as an athlete, an entertainer, a drug dealer, a gangster and a goon. Again, you may acknowledge your sons intelligence when he brings home the report card every quarter; finishing the year with A's and B's. However, for 13 years (K-12), 180 days per year, 8 hours per day, he is picked on, criticized and disrespected for his intelligence. It is just a matter of time before he gives in. And yes, I know we can say that he must be stronger than that. However, if an adult cannot resist the temptation to cheat in a workplace romance, how much more can a child stand firm when they are continually being disrespected under similar pressures for a much longer time? Let it marinate.

It begins first with one of the first attacks from his peers. That attack being the association that being smart is acting white. This sets the tone and lays the ground work for all to follow. First, because our schools tend to be "urban" and the demographic predominantly looks like us. So this in essence, can outcast the child under the notion that his form of Black isn't Black; therefore it isn't embraced or respected. However, the child does see what forms are respected and continuously reaffirmed to garner respect. Those being the athlete, the entertainer, the drug dealer, the gangster and the goon. The athlete, entertainer and goon are more in the early years of schooling. The drug dealers and gangsters emerge more in the later years of life. Allow me to explain the inception and the reaffirmation of the Black boy's respect.

The most obvious and prevalent is the athlete. Many of us and our boys could run a route and shoot a basketball before we learned to comprehend what we read. Simply because that is generally the way many of our parents think boys should be. It's so cliché but it's well ingrained. So ingrained that it seems like a rites of passage. This is an aspect, as boys, that we learned received respect. The moment we get "good" at it, the seed is planted that we can make it to the league. Our feeling of respect is increased when we become admired for our physical ability. The fastest kid in the third grade, that fourth grader with the sick handles. Those monikers garner respect from our peers. As we get better, the admiration leads to popularity. Popularity that leads to being picked first in kick ball or the next 5 on 5 at recess. As an adult, it seems frivolous. However, as a child it becomes so much more. It's respect. Remember, respect is to men what love is to women. When I get respected as an athlete, I strive to be more athletic.

But here's where it becomes deeper and problematic. My athleticism gets me 1st place and MVP trophies while only needing a C average to play sports. I also receive articles in the newspaper and attention from everyone in the school. As an athlete, I even receive a level of respect from the teachers as an asset to the school. Such an asset that teachers will pass me simply because they know I can play the game well enough to not "need" the education. I go on to receive full ride scholarships for playing sports. Go to college, respect increases; popularity becomes mild fame. I go from newspapers to news channels. I bring revenue to the university because I'm a walking highlight. Then that fatal turn of events occurs. No, not THAT one. The one where I face that injury that I can't recover from. The coach cuts me from the team. The teachers stop passing me. The popularity fizzes out. I have about 2 years left in school and have no clue what to do with my life or this Business Administration degree when I get out. The respect begins to dissipate because I no longer have what was used to earn it; therefore, the respect is no longer given. However, the nerd in school we ragged on for being corny and unable to catch because he kept a book in his hand is now the man that I'm interviewing for.

Of course, this is a very dramatic extreme. But how many of us are in a similar position? More so, how many of us are in this position where we feel that our son will be the saving grace to rise where we fell? See how this subtle cycle works so smoothly? It's all in what we deem deserving of respect. The error was never in the injury. It was in the lack of respect toward intellect and intelligence. If this is not an ideology in the mind of the adult, it cannot become an ideology in the mind of the child. Black boys should not have to wait until they are Black men to be respected by Black people for their intelligence. Just as we respected, acknowledged and honored LeBron before he entered the league, we need to keep that same energy for the little scholars whose minds are the impetus for our evolution. Otherwise, we continue the path for athletes and entertainers to emerge and set the precedence for a Black boy's respect.

When it comes to entertainment, there are two types specific to this writing. Comedians and Rappers/Singers.

Entertainment receives respect because it can capture the mind and soul in ways many things cannot. From an etymological sense, the word entertainment can be broken down to the prefix enter-, meaning to go into; the root –tain-, meaning to hold/take; and the suffix –ment, meaning the mind. The word entertainment means to go into and hold the mind. So be careful when you say, "It's jUSt entErtaINment." More so when you are easily entertained. But I digress.

The comedian comes to light as the class clown. His respect is granted through the laughter of his peers. That laughter fuels him and pushes him further. It pushes him even more if he can ever get his teacher to laugh or the adults he involves himself with to crack a smile. Here's where this gets deeper. There are generally two types of comedy that our people seem to connect with. These types are either satirical or buffoonery. The satirical style of comedy uses intellect and wit to convey humor. This form of comedy is also the basis for sarcasm. When a comedic child uses satirical humor, they can often be viewed as disrespectful because the person they are speaking to feels they are insulting their intelligence. The reality to that is the child is simply responding in accordance with what was given to them. These children are generally not comedians; just really funny people. Yet in a hierarchical system, they are deemed rude to people when they are really being reflective.

The other comedic style is buffoonery. This form of comedy is the most revered form. Comedians of this nature tend to be excessively vocal and physically active to express the joke or make people laugh; often using many facial expressions and gestures. Because this style is more respected (from movies, T.V. and social media), this is the one most embodied by our sons in schools; until it backfires, that is. It backfires because we disrupt class and we cannot sit still; serving as the impetus which will segue into ADHD. We randomly make noises and break out into dance. Yes, for attention; but more for the respect associated with this expression of entertainment. Again, respect is to men what love is to women. I'll take a write up and a whooping for the respect that I'll receive from the people who laugh at my antics 8 hours a day, 5 days a week, 180 days a year. Why? Because I'm just as funny as the greats; imitating everything I see them do in their specials. No, I don't, and shouldn't, know better than what entertains you as an adult. After all, we watch it together as you laugh until your eyes water. Yet, you tell me that I'm wrong for exhibiting the exact behavior? Remember, a child's behavior is not a product of right and wrong but of habit and normalcy. The normalcy which entertains the parent will serve as the template for how their child will entertain the world; which segues into the next form of entertainment.

When we consider rappers and singers as forms of entertainment, we must consider that these dynamics are among the most glorified expressions next to athletes. The rappers are more respected by our brothers and the singers by our sisters. The chosen path of artistry is contingent upon environment, skill and acknowledgement. Environment being which type of music was most dominant in the home. Most rappers grew up on rap, jazz and funk music; most singers grew up on R&B, soul and gospel. Skill is basically if a note or harmony could be held, for a singer; or if a flow could be recited, for a rapper. The acknowledgement is the pivotal point. Was the practice encouraged or shunned? That will aide in dictating if the stage is set for our sons to seek respect through this medium. For the sake of the writing, we will assume that it was encouraged.

Before I go further, let me express that I am not against rapping/singing. For some of our sons, that is their gift. The very thing they were placed in this world to give to the masses. Some of them have the divine ability of word play and verbalization (rapper) and some have the divine ability of unlimited range and vocal control. However, when this gift obtains respect through the medium of toxic femininity, their gift becomes a curse. This curse then leads to the destruction of themselves and our people. Not because their music is inherently bad; but because the promoted music is inherently bad. From a level of divinity, music utilizes the aritu (chakra) element of sound by placing mantras over instrumentation in the form of song. This sound is looped continuously until the words pass the subconscious mind to enter the unconscious mind. The subconscious mind is where the words are stored. This is how you are able to know all the words without remembering when you learned them. The unconscious mind is where the energy of the song is stored. This is how you are able to act out the behavior of the song's lyrics. This is why we must be cognizant of which songs we allow to be "our shits" because they eventually become the "shit" we start embodying. This is why Fuck The Police caught backlash while songs creating a thousand ways to kill a nigga are circulating the airways. But I digress.

When we consider that our sons are acknowledged for being rappers/singers, we have to view the respect factor in accordance with toxic femininity. The songs most heavily circulated have destructive mantras in them; both rap/hip hop and R&B. Hip Hop has multiple layers that will be discussed a little later. R&B on the other hand has two main focuses: sex and misogyny. Obviously, sex is

the point of baby making music. Misogyny, as
alluded to in So Frail, is the competition
between men. If you truly analyze the
mainstream R&B music sang by Black men,
you will either hear how good we are at sex
and making love or how much better we are
for a woman than her current man. Just take a
second to think about your favorite male R&B
artists and their catalogues of hits. Feel me?
The catalogues are entirely too broad for this
to be a simple coincidence. Put a pin in this as
we move to the rap side; tying them both
together later.

When it comes to the rap side, there
are far more layers to the destructive mantras
layered over the instruments. In one of his
interviews, Tupac said, "…if niggas got little
nuts, it's gonna start getting' back to a
different type of rap. Partyin' and fuckin' and
all that type shit because that's what we talk
about when they don't let us talk about what
we really wanna talk about." That's a pivotal

73

quote because it encompasses the current and most recent state of rap music. But the questions are how and why? How, because toxic femininity fuels the mentality that generates the destruction. Why, because that gets respect within the culture and community. The current layers of mainstream rap are murder, drugs, sex, misogynoir and dumb shit. I wish I had a means to truly define that last layer but dumb shit is all it really is. There is nothing but inconsistent and incoherent thoughts over dope beats. Real quick, let's return to the aritu associated with sound. When inconsistent and incoherent mantras penetrate the subconscious mind and enter the unconscious mind, what can you expect to be embodied by the listener? Furthermore, how much more potent does it become when this is where the respect is coming from? How deadlier is it when toxic femininity is its fuel? Yea. Its only entertainment. Now let's bring it all together.

When our sons are earning their respect through the mode of entertainment, specifically music, the first seed is nurtured by the manner in which we respond to their perception. The music we listen to most is the normalcy and habit that will lead them into their respective path. Going deeper, the artists we listen to and recite the most are the artists they will emulate as well (Lil' Wayne single handedly changed an entire era of rap to be him); simply because, as a parent, we respect this particular expression which our sons will interpret as the medium that will grant them respect as well. Music is much more potent because of the manner in which it hits the unconscious mind. When the unconscious mind is penetrated, the energy will fuel the behavior embodied through the music of the songs. Every time our sons sing along, they are reaffirming the mantras that are embedding certain mentalities into their psyches. This effect is so much easier because it is accepted that this receives respect from my parents; therefore, I should receive respect as well. As time passes, they decide they want to take rapping/singing seriously and begin working on their mixtape. The moment we finally hear our sons' music, what does it generally embody? The money, drugs, misogynoir, sex and dumb shit. Why? Because it earns respect. The one thing, as men, we thrive for. As I said before, respect is to men what love is to women. We will earn it how we see fit.

The next expression of our respect is the basis for the final two expressions. That expression being the goon. With maturation, the goon will transform into the gangster and/or drug dealer. In many regards, gangsters and drug dealers are one and the same. However, not all drug dealers are gangsters and not all gangsters are drug dealers; contrary to mainstream media. Gangsters are more so into violent crimes;

76

hence the need to move in silence. Drug dealers are into violent crimes, as necessary, but are typically operable within nonviolent parameters; the "successful" ones operating as businessmen, more or less. Despite the divergence between the two, their origin derives from the common point of being a goon.

The goon can be labeled as a soldier, a rider, a lil homie, etc. Euphemisms aside, the goon is the manifestation of a rugged exterior with a careless and reckless mentality. This is a mentality that is established in childhood by two specific points. The first being "fight fight" and the second being "stop being a punk." As simple as these points are, and as harmless as they appear, we are turning our sons into emotionless beings who lack the ability to feel and comprehend through rationale.

Understand that I am not saying do not teach them to defend themselves or to be soft.

What I am saying is that there needs to be structure and purpose behind why we are telling them to fight and why we encourage them to be tough. Too many times we are promoting "fight fight" in the sense of playtime. This is poisonous because we are setting the standard for them to internalize that inflicting pain is a means of recreation. This is intensified because we laugh and smile with them during the behavior. Their subconscious minds don't internalize good or bad. Their minds see normalcy. Normalcy that doesn't have meaning or structure to it. We are not teaching them what to fight for, when to fight and who they should be fighting. The only instruction they have with "fight fight" is that if someone hits you, you hit them back. What do you think this does to a child who internalizes "fight fight" as playtime with the instructions of you hit me, I hit you? Sit with that one because it gets deeper.

To couple the "fight fight" premise with the "don't be a punk" philosophy is the icing on the cake. That ideology comes by, first, telling a child not to cry and/or fix their face and second, telling them that "it didn't even hurt that bad" or that they will be alright. Hear me well with this one. What you, as an adult, are telling a child, your child, is that they are not really feeling what they are feeling; and if they are, they need to stop feeling it. In real time, you are teaching them that their pain is not real; that it is an illusion to them. When we add the spiritual component, all children view life as a reflection and that people feel and experience things as they do. When they inflict pain, they cannot perceive that the person's pains are real because their pains "didn't hurt that bad" and that person will be alright. After years of this conditioning, the son is replaced by the goon who really doesn't give a fuck.

When I don't give a fuck, yet I still want respect, guess what I grow up into? A being who can kill and inflict pain without as much as a wink because it doesn't hurt that bad; gangster. Or a being who can administer poison to his people because they will be alright; drug dealer. Either way, I'm respected. And respect is to men what love it to women. When my respect is granted through the lens of toxic femininity, I am unapologetically destructive with the power I now possess. We really need to redefine how our boys are respected and default them with the respect they deserve.

POWER WITHOUT STRENGTH

"These leaders got power but they all lack strength." I wrote that line at a time when a lot of volatile circumstances were occurring amongst my people. There were red hats and oval office meetings, perms and selfies, Quaaludes and pudding, you name it. The "leaders" proved to have no strength when it all came down to it. In the heat of the moment, they served more as pacifiers than activists. Understand this is not to discredit ANY of their individual contributions to the culture. However, their contributions do not absolve them of accountability. Furthermore, the liberation of the individual can be catalyzed by a leader but it belongs to the individual. We must always remember that people are people. No matter what their position of power is, we will never know the capacity of their strength. We need to be our own leaders and saviors in accordance with our own divinity. Nothing can save you but you; should you accept both your power and strength.

In the words of Huey Newton, "...power is, first of all, the ability to define phenomena and the ability to make the phenomena act in a desired manner." Strength is the capacity to continually exert power against resistance and opposition until that capacity is reached or the resistance stops; whichever comes first. When both of these definitions are overstood in conjunction with one another, we can easily observe how that line about our current leaders is a reality. They make phenomena act in a certain way but it's not exerted against resistance; instead it's with resistance. This lack of strength is a direct result of toxic femininity; which leads to destruction. Destruction of morals, destruction of principles, destruction of legacies and the destruction of the people.

The destruction is not always of the physical manifestation of desecration and dilapidation. It is of the mental and spiritual manifestation of passivism, cowardice and fear. When a "leader" is "awarded" power within a particular scope, there are expectations that must be met; consistently. Expectations of the allies and expectations of the enemies. Obviously, the allies support and the enemies resist the power; as they should. The issue comes from the strength, or lack thereof, of the wielders of said power. When the strength begins to dwindle, the enemies infiltrate and the allies withdraw. This sets the tone for the manner and direction in which the power will move.

There is a saying that "everyone has a price." This is a very true statement and is directly connected to power. There is always a price to pay for the power that one obtains. Strength takes this idea a step further. Although there is always a price, only select currencies can and will be accepted. No exceptions. This is epitomized in the phrase "the strength to endure." In matters of power, the strength to endure must outlast all temptation, coercion and manipulation. When the strength to endure outlasts resistance, masculinity will reign supreme. When the strength to endure falters, toxic femininity emerges. The greatest example of both sides of this power and strength connection occurs between two specific comedic greats who will, culturally, remain icons forever. However, one emerges with his strength and the other emerges without it; more or less. Coincidentally, the one who maintained his strength continuously has his image tarnished while the one who no longer has his strength is glorified continually.

Although both, inherently, became "mainstream" through stereotypically expressions, their styles of comedy were completely polarized. One leveraged his persona as a pimp to provide a satirical form of comedy that was relatively conscious about the world through a cultural dynamic. The other leveraged a culturally accepted persona of buffoonery to provide a style of comedy based on self-ridicule and personal humiliation. In their respective careers, both reached amazing heights. However, at some point, one plateaued and the other propelled to what is deemed "super stardom" in the eyes of mainstream entertainment. Coincidence? You be the judge on that. An interpretation of these two comedians is a very relevant example of the dynamics of the power and strength connection.

In So Frail, I included a chapter titled "Oh, My Goodness!!!" That chapter was a driving force for this second installment. It speaks on the ways many Black male celebrities are castrated. The information of that chapter will be used as a defining piece of this specific power and strength connection. Although I could have easily used Malcolm and Martin, I personally feel that we need to move on from that dynamic. Never forget or undermine them, but move forward from constantly revisiting them as the points of reference because we are no longer living in that time. In fact, we are living in the time manifested through Martin's power and absent strength eclipsing Malcolm's power and present strength. This led to integration; which ultimately sets the tone for how this example plays out. By no means am I comparing these men to Malcolm and Martin. However, the principles are relevant and very consistent between the two dynamics.

By referencing the "Oh, My Goodness!!!" chapter, it's obvious that I will be discussing the comedian who falls into that dynamic and how this relates to the power and strength connection. I remember when this brother was on the rise and he was given the leading role in a very stereotypical movie. This movie was, in many ways, his "breakout" moment into mainstream entertainment. The movie, of course, brought about much clout and notoriety. This, of course, would lead to interviews, speaking engagements, etc. It also leads to a very specific point in a Black comedian's career. That point being the infamous "wearing of the dress." Strangely enough, it seems to be the point where the careers take off; exponentially.

I remember watching this brother in an interview post-stereotypical movie and pre-blowup. In this interview he was asked if he would ever put on a dress. In that moment, with a straight face and eyes of conviction he stated, "No. I will never put on a dress." You could see the power in his eyes and feel it in his words. I believe that he genuinely meant that at the time in which he spoke those words. However, something occurred after that moment that was able to change his mind. Sometime down the line, he performed a skit on a popular late night television show in which he wore a purple dress. Within that moment, and beyond, his career took off to astronomical heights. Special after special, movie after movie, he was really soaring; gaining more power. But was he losing strength?

I asked that question because he had an interview that touched on the incident with the dress. In this interview he laughed as he discussed the clip showing him saying he would never wear a dress followed by him in a dress. He made light of the situation alluding to the fact that "things change and things happen." But what exactly are these things? And just how do they happen? Those questions I cannot answer. What I can answer is that whatever it is, the resistance exceeded the strength. So much so that many of his roles since then have included him braiding a man's hair in the movie promo, kissing men, whining and being thrown around like a rag doll. I get that it is "comedy." But is it, really? Or as the "Oh, My Goodness!!!" chapter alludes, is it a further means of emasculation by gaining power in the absence of strength? That question is left for you to answer. Please, comprehend that there is no such thing as coincidence; and my brother has his power but lacks his strength.

On the other side of that coin is power with strength. As stated before, the other comedian also gained mainstream notoriety through a stereotypical means. He is culturally acknowledged as the funny pimp; creating his platform and fan base primarily on being a pimp. Whether a movie pimp or a cartoon pimp, he's been a pimp. However, despite his stereotypical expression, his comedy possesses intelligent subliminals covered in a basic presentation. His jokes ranged from politics to pop culture and everything in between. He possesses the gift of comedy; not just the ability to make people laugh. Which, in turn, is where his power resides.

I must be honest here. For a time, I looked at this brother through tainted filters. There was a time when it seemed that his career stopped and he just vanished when he was at his peak. The first experience I remember was randomly seeing a mugshot of him. The media then spun that he was "going crazy" as he was all smiles in the mugshot. The he would go on to have repeated "run ins with the law." One thing that always stuck out was that he was smiling in these mugshots. At the time, my thought was that he was really going crazy and the fame got to him. Then one day I heard him "break his silence" and explain his run ins. It changed my perspective on that and him.

In both an interview and a comedy special he stated that, and I'm paraphrasing, "they are fuckin' with me because I won't break. For every time you've seen me arrested, I've never been convicted." When he said that, I had to stop and think back. He was right. He was never convicted; which is why he smiled in the mugshots and courtroom pictures. In modern terms, he was unbothered. As it pertains to this writing, his strength remained intact. Things didn't change or happen. He never compromised. So much so that he owns all of the masters to his specials and takes all profits with no one to pay or answer to. The resistance is futile to him as his strength to endure far exceeds the resistance.

With these two examples of the power and strength connection, it is evident that there is something missing from many of our "leaders" and a distinct differentiation between the two "heads" operating in a given space at a given time. I mentioned Martin and Malcolm already. There's also W.E.B. DuBois and Booker T. Washington. Hell, we saw it with Biggie and Pac; Bad Boy and Death Row. One side accepting their power but lacking strength and following the mainstream by assimilation. The other side accepting their power and maintaining their strength; realizing the idea of for self, by self. Refusing to integrate into a system they did not create. This possession of power in the absence of strength is the position accepted by many Black "leaders" today. They prefer a seat at the table of an oppressive feast over a feast at home. When this is infused with toxic femininity, the destruction of the mind and soul is established. One's ability to face adversity, stand firm in their morals and fight for their strength to be greater than the resistance is obsolete. Once that ability is obsolete, the subsequent generations accept this as reality as it imprints into their subconscious minds; suppressing their masculinity forever to permanently function through toxic femininity.

CONSCIOUS IMPRINTS

There are three modalities to the mind.
The conscious mind, the subconscious mind
and the unconscious mind. Just as the mind is
the bridge between the body and the soul, so
too, is the subconscious mind the bridge
between the conscious and unconscious
minds. The conscious mind is the biased mind
that ingests the information we gather. The
subconscious mind is the semi-biased mind
that digests that gathered information. The
unconscious mind is the unbiased mind that
assimilates and distributes the information
that will penetrate and imprint the soul.
Contrary to popular belief, the unconscious
mind is not a dormant or inactive state of

mind. In fact, it is the most active and is responsible for our habitual, automatic and instinctive actions. Knowing and fully comprehending this understanding is pivotal in observing how toxic femininity becomes the expression that overrides masculinity; our natural predisposition.

The conscious mind is the biased mind. This is the realm where knowledge and information reside. This modality of the mind is biased because it selectively allows information in. Information that is only in alignment with personal values and morals. I say selective because our conscious mind points us towards experiences and opportunities that are part of our particular plan in life. For example, when one decides that they desire a career in medicine what do they do? They choose a school with a strong Pre-Med program that fits their values and morals. They choose something close to home but not too close. They want to avoid out of state costs as much as possible. While in the program, they shadow physicians, take prerequisite courses, study for the MCAT, apply for schools and complete internships. These are all proponents of their conscious mind. They are obtaining the knowledge and information as it pertains to this consciously directed path. This is selective and biased because the focus is solely around obtaining the knowledge to complete the goal, more or less. But an important part to completing the goal is to apply the knowledge and transform it into wisdom.

Wisdom resides in the subconscious mind. The subconscious mind is the modality that is semi-biased because it is semi-selective to the information it receives. The conscious mind allows information that correlates to personal values and morals. The subconscious mind allows the information that correlates to the information that correlates to personal values and morals. In sticking with the example of a career in medicine, once the conscious mind has been calibrated to this path, the subconscious mind opens up to all things that revolve around this calibration. For example, this student learns medical terminology; studying it daily. The student goes home for a holiday break and their family is watching a show on their favorite health channel. In passing for a snack, on the phone with a friend from school, they hear "...potential drug overdose. Patient entered with tachycardia and pyrexia. We need to move fast..." The student perks up and catches tachycardia and pyrexia from their studies. They then say, "Tachycardia and pyrexia? That's a fast heartbeat and a fever. What kind of drug did they take?"

This student's subconscious mind picked up on the terminology because it was information that correlated to the information that correlated to their personal values and morals. The conscious mind no longer needed to be active for that information because the knowledge was applied and transformed into wisdom. This wisdom made the student fully aware of the circumstance without being "aware" at all; since they were talking to the friend from school. When knowledge becomes wisdom through application, all that is ingested by the conscious mind becomes digested by the subconscious mind. From the digestion of the subconscious mind comes the assimilation and distribution by the unconscious mind.

Allow me to reiterate that the unconscious mind is not an inactive, dormant state of mind. The unconscious mind is the "pilot" when we are in autopilot. Just as the conscious and subconscious minds house knowledge and wisdom, respectively, the unconscious mind houses understanding. Understanding is the application of wisdom. To apply knowledge makes one wise; to apply wisdom makes one understanding. To understand grants the ability to act and/or react without thinking. As previously mentioned, this is where habit and instinct reside; specifically instinct. In sticking with the career in medicine example, I will tie in how the unconscious mind works.

The student has completed medical school and has begun their residency program. They are currently in their ER rotation. This particular night, the ER is short staffed (for the purpose of the example) and the resident is put on notice that they will be needed in crunch time. No sooner than the notice is made, three patients enter the emergency room as victims of a mall shooting. Two are stable with nonlethal wounds. The other is in critical condition and must be rushed to surgery immediately. The patient's heart rate is dropping rapidly and they are bleeding profusely. The attending physician looks to the resident and says, "He's losing a lot of blood and will need an immediate transfusion." The resident nods and sprints away; returning with several blood packs of Type O blood, sterilized IV needles, IV tubing adapters and alcohol wipes. The resident immediately sterilized the area of the available arm, inserts the IV and connects the blood bag; hanging it above the patients head as the attending physician gets the bleeding under control and stabilizes the patient. The patient pulls through. The resident has saved the patient's life because the unconscious mind took over.

The unconscious mind is where understanding is housed. It is also the unbiased modality of the mind that is strengthened by the application of wisdom. Wisdom is also a derivative of experience. In essence, understanding is also the application of experience. This is how this all ties in. When the attending told the resident "He's losing a lot of blood and will need an immediate transfusion," no instructions were given. However, the resident knew to go to the blood bank and exactly which route to take because they understood the layout of the hospital by frequently traveling the floors. The resident knew to get type O blood bags, multiple, because 1) type O is the universal donor and there was no time to find out the patient's blood type and 2) with profuse bleeding there was no telling when the bleeding would be controlled. The resident also knew to retrieve IV needles, tubing and sterilizing wipes to initiate the transfusion. Once arrived, the resident paced the IV in the arm, connected the blood and helped save the patient's life. But how was all of this understood between the attending saying, "He's losing a lot of blood" and the resident nodding, sprinting off? The unconscious mind was in action.

The unconscious mind understood what the physician spoke without having to think about it. It simply caused the entire being to act. From the head nod to the IV needles, the resident knew exactly what to do because the knowledge was obtained, applied and transformed to wisdom. The wisdom was the experiences applied and transformed into understanding. This understanding lead to instinctive action that the resident just knew to do without dwelling on the pressure or the emotion of the circumstance. The unconscious mind, through the synergy with the conscious and subconscious minds, created an outcome through unbiased thought that, in this case, saved a life.

So now the question is, "if this is about toxic femininity, what was the purpose of using the career in medicine? That doesn't seem to be a result of toxic femininity." Although that could be true, the example was used to dissect the conscious, subconscious and unconscious minds through a positive dynamic while simultaneously providing the intersectionality of the patient in critical condition needing the transfusions being a casualty of toxic femininity. Now that you have the understanding of the conscious, unconscious and subconscious minds, it will be easier to understand how toxic femininity infuses within our psyches.

For this expression, I will paint this scenario as if it were a blank canvas. By now we are all aware of the perpetual cycles so I won't beat a dead horse. If you've read So Frail, you're familiar with the residual effects of slavery. Recall from previous chapters how toxic femininity is catalyzed by the school to prison pipeline, respect and "leaders" with power and no strength. From beginning to end, I will show how these points catalyzed the toxic femininity that led to the patient in critical care being saved by the resident.

Now, this example is hypothetical and all of our sons do not have this experience, obviously. However, when our sons are murdered in the streets, the "theme" seems to be that they were thugs, criminals or gangsters that caused the overse...I mean the officer to fear for his life. Since that's a common narrative, I won't shy away from it here. I will also show how this narrative is able to be used if you're able to catch it.

As now familiarized, the conscious mind is the biased mind that ingests the information. A young Black king is growing up in a society that has a preconceived perception about him. His consciousness accepts this as he witnesses and begins observing the information of his surroundings. His parents have "the talk" with him to insure that he knows he is a target in a system designed to oppose him where he must work twice as hard for half as much. Within his surroundings he absorbs music that promotes criminal behavior, views television programs that promote dysfunction and irrationality, and observes daily interactions between men who resemble him that express "manly" tendencies limited to sex, money and drugs; both subtly and grossly. He sees news stories of people who resemble him being murdered by police and "vigilantes" and witnesses events outside of his door where people who look like him are murdered by their reflections. This begins to shape his mentality as his conscious mind is being programmed to internalize toxic femininity as masculinity. This now creates the biased lens that filters his perception because this is all he sees; therefore it's all he accepts as his normalcy.

From this normalcy comes his semi-biased observations through the subconscious mind that digests this gathered information. His applied information, unanimously dubbed street smarts, is the wisdom that allows his subconscious mind to function. This functioning allows his friendships to develop through normalcy and cultural internalization. As stated before, the subconscious mind is associated with the information that correlates with the information that correlates to personal values and morals. This allows him to be open to friendships and lifestyles that resonate with him and feel normal to him within a given context; more or less. His friends will hold true to many of the standards bestowed upon him. And this is the point where toxic femininity begins to infuse.

He, and his friends, will dress a certain way, talk a certain way, listen to certain music, watch certain television shows, etc. The issue with this, and how it pertains to the subconscious mind, is that these things are subtly observed. Just as the resident randomly picked up the words tachycardia and pyrexia while being on the phone, so will the young king pick up the subtleties digested within his subconscious mind. But just what are these subtleties? His favorite song has infused within him that he is a goon who pops pills and sips lean. His favorite social media troll sips lean, listens to that same music and does random acts of theft and finessing. The friends in his circle listen to this same music and conduct these same activities. He is friends with them because his subconscious mind has been calibrated to that frequency. Like a moth to a flame, he easily gravitates to it. Through repetition, it multiplies and strengthens. Through relationships, it solidifies as this becomes the lifestyle he lives out because the wisdom of his subconscious mind has been applied to become understanding in the unconscious mind.

Here is the moment where it all comes together. The young king has now reached the level of understanding that allows his unconscious mind to lead him in regards to his lifestyle. Toxic femininity infused and dominated his masculinity; causing his analysis and deconstructive faculties to be overridden by the toxic expressions of his synthesis and constructive faculties. When the feminine faculties are toxic, creation becomes destruction. This young king has now patterned his life according to toxic feminine behavior. One step further, he has established friendships rooted in the toxic behavior. This behavior is strengthened and reaffirmed through his music, his role models and daily entertainment; as they are all calibrated toward the toxic feminine manifestation of the life he lives that was previously solidified in his subconscious mind. Now it is acted out by his unconscious mind.

So the young king and two of his friends decide to partake in the senseless behavior glorified in the music they hear and amplified by the media they see. They double cup the lean and pop a few xans. The three hit up the mall to scheme on some shoppers with the intent of snatching bags from the first person they see. No ifs, ands or maybes about it. They post up outside of the food court for their victim. A middle aged sister walks out of

the food court with three bags. The three spot
her and begin to move. The young king says,
"Y'all, let's chill. This shit don't feel right."
One of the friends says, "Quit being a bitch
and come on. This is gang shit breh." So the
three continue walking toward the woman.
She spots them and picks up her pace; moving
swiftly towards a black charger with black
tints. One of the friends says, "Oh, shit. This
is about to be a mean liq." They move faster
towards her and she begins to run. They laugh
and begin to jog. One of the friends says,
"...bitch really think she's about to get
away." At that moment, the woman screams,
"BAAABYY!!!" and the door of the charger
opens up. Within a split second, 10 shots fired
from the charger toward the three. They could
not run fast enough and they were all hit. Two
were left stable with nonlethal wounds. The
young king was in critical condition and
needed to be rushed to surgery immediately.

His heart rate was dropping rapidly and he was bleeding profusely.

Although this is an extreme circumstance, I hope the principles are recognized and understood. The conscious mind is the biased mind that ingests information. The subconscious mind is the semi-biased mind that digests the information. The unconscious mind is the unbiased mind that assimilates and distributes the information that will penetrate and imprint the soul. Once it hits the soul, it dictates the will. Recall from So Frail, the body, mind and soul create a synergy between action, thought and will, respectively. The body performs the actions that are created by the thoughts which are invoked by the will which is strengthened by continued action. With the mind (thought) being the bridge between the body (action) and the soul (will), once the unconscious mind has been programmed, the actions that require no thought to complete are easily willed. When this programming is structured to express toxic femininity, the soul will invoke the thoughts to make this a reality. A reality to Black male masculinity. As long as we believe that what we exhibit is masculinity, we cannot make the necessary change to shatter the illusion. Therefore, to change our being, we must acknowledge our conscious imprints to rectify that dynamic. The most pivotal and foundational way to do that is to harmonize with women; our women.

(WHY) BITCHES AIN'T SHIT

By now, we're pretty familiar with
what toxic femininity is and many of the
things that cause it. We are also aware that
despite sharing the polarity of femininity,
women hold the predisposition for it. We
have observed what type of men are
manifested within the dynamic of toxic
femininity. With all of these things being
considered, we now face the impetus and fuel
behind why bitches ain't shit. This is the
affirmation that personifies the clashes
between the dynamics of femininity; toxic
versus healthy.

Before I go further, I am not
defaulting that all women express healthy

femininity and all men have a toxic femininity. I am speaking solely on the interaction that occurs between the two dynamics of femininity. I do not refer to women as bitches. However, there seems to be a distinct correlation between the feminine component, the feminine gender and the word bitch. In casual conversation, we refer to women as bitches. In casual conversation, women refer to themselves as bitches. When men and women become argumentative we say, "quit bitchin'." When emotions are heavily involved, both men and women say, "Quit acting like a bitch." This correlation brought about the understanding found within the principles that reside beneath the details of the word bitch. With this understanding, I will show why bitches ain't shit and how it pertains to toxic femininity.

Bitches ain't shit is a historic principle established with misogyny. Misogyny is an idea that has evolved into the hatred of women through its inception as the competition between men. The "champion" is the one who can take the "trophy" from his competitor. In all dynamics the greatest "trophy" a man can obtain is a woman. This is universally accepted in all facets of nature. From the mating rituals of birds to the mating calls of coyotes, it inevitably ends with the man obtaining the woman; in the most basic and carnal dynamic. When we add the premise of genetics; alpha, beta and epsilon males; and a functioning brain, we begin to see how the competition evolves into rivalry. The rivalry evolves into hatred; the hatred creates doctrines that codify and justify the subjugation of the men outside of the doctrine through a falsified superiority complex. This subjugation, by default, trickles down to the women and the children. This subjugation is transformed into oppression that is ordained by specific deities. These deities then "grant" the oppressors the ability to conquer lands;

slaughter men, women, children and cattle while keeping the virgins for themselves. This transformation of the competition between men evolves into the hatred of women and continues to multiply.

The first two points to this inception are genetics and alpha, beta and epsilon males. Genetically, there are only three races of people. The Africoid, the Mongoloid and the Caucasoid. Contrary to popular propaganda, we all are not the "same on the inside." Phenotypically, there is a specific distinction between the races in cranial structure alone. Genotypically, the distinctions are astronomical in measure. This also leads to the differences within the mind and the soul; as the body, mind and soul are one synergistic entity. This is not a means to promote division or derision. This is simply expressing what nature has presented to us all.

When we consider genetics, we must consider the Punnett square. The basic point of this four block square overtly shows the genetic types while covertly showing the distinction between the races of people. The genetic types are homozygous and heterozygous; with the distinctions being dominant and recessive. The Punnett square breaks this down to homozygous dominant (YY), heterozygous dominant (Yy), heterozygous recessive (yY) and homozygous recessive (yy). We can juxtapose this with the three races as follows: the Africoid race is homozygous dominant (YY). The Caucasoid race is homozygous recessive (yy). The Mongoloid race is heterozygous with the divergence of heterozygous dominant (Yy) being closer to the Africoid race and heterozygous recessive (yY) being closer to the Caucasoid race. From this expression, we can observe, through natural design, what the juxtaposition will be for the alpha, beta and epsilon genetic templates are.

The alpha, beta and epsilon expression was detailed in So Frail as it pertains to my brothers. I will not revisit that dynamic here. However, this particular depiction is necessary for the purposes of this chapter. Through natural design, the homozygous dominant template is associated with the alpha, the heterozygous template is associate with the beta and the homozygous recessive template is associated with the epsilon. The reason gamma and delta were skipped was explained in So Frail. Again, I will not repeat that here; as it will disrupt the flow of the writing.

According to the manner in which the genetic templates have been naturally laid out, the distinctions between the templates have been clear phenotypically and genotypically. If you recall, the body, the mind and the soul are one; operating within a synergistic fashion. This means that the manner in which the genetics are physically depicted, so too will be the mind and the soul. These points of being will also reside in the same alpha, beta and epsilon expressions. This means that the mentality and spirituality will also have distinctions between the three races of people.

The third point to the inception of misogyny as the competition between men stems from the functioning brain. A functioning brain that separates humans from animals by means of higher order thinking. Remember that mentality falls into the same alignment of alpha, beta and epsilon. Mentality is the realm for our thinking space and the point where we create and manipulate thoughts. As it pertains to mentality and this writing, I will specifically speak on the word race; as it has significance for this dynamic of the writing.

Race, as it has been associated today, represents the genetics of the human species. However, this definition was first used in the year 1580. Race was originally defined in the

14th century as a competition of speed. Key word: competition. When we understand these definitions, we must observe that race, in its full capacity, is the competition between the genetics of the human species. This competition will then be between the alpha, beta and epsilon depictions of the genetic expressions. Taking this one step further, we get the competition between the Africoid, the Mongoloid and the Caucasoid. Now, I am well aware that it hasn't been expressed why bitches ain't shit. Hang tight; it's coming. This is all necessary.

So we've spoken on the physical and mental. Now we incorporate the spiritual so it can all make sense going forward. There is a very pivotal point in history that is considered to be the changing of the guards, so to speak. This transition of "power" occurs in a moment when, our-storically, Kemet becomes Egypt and his-storically, the baton passes from the Egyptians to the Hebrews to the

119

Greeks to the Romans. It is at this moment that spirituality becomes religion, allegorical metaphors become literal events and Kemetic iconography becomes Abrahamic religion. It is this transition in which man born of the womb becomes woman crafted from a rib. This is the first instance in which women were stripped of their natural divinity. It is also the point where misogyny comes full circle as the competition between men and the hatred of women.

The Abrahamic religions, coincidentally the three major religions, are Judaism, Christianity and Islam. Each tend to follow the same theme from the time of Adam up until Shem and Abraham. With Abraham comes the divergence as Ishmael was born of Hagar and Isaac was born of Sarah. Isaac will become the impetus for Judaism and Christianity and Ishmael will become the impetus for Islam. The main focus of each religion is the centered theme that the children of the religions are the chosen people. I'm not here to argue about who was chosen and who wasn't; who wrote what, what should be followed or even how it fits into history. My stance is specifically catered to misogyny. The competition between men and the hatred of women; and how this all ties in.

First, whether or not the original authors or people were Black is of no concern to me because the current wielders of the copyrights and publishing of the doctrines belong to those of the recessive expressions of genetics; the Caucasian and the Arab. Furthermore, those beings used these very doctrines to enslave the Africoid race at some point in their history. The Trans/Sub-Saharan slave trade was justified by Islam and created kaffirs. The Trans-Atlantic slave trade was justified by Christianity /Judaism and created niggers. The ideology of the doctrines implied the superiority of the men by implying superiority of the deities. This superiority of deities developed the notion that a "chosen people" from a relatively small radius between Israel, Egypt and Jerusalem were inevitably set above, and given dominion over the rest of the people of the world. This is the manner in which the tone is set for the competition between men. When the epsilon stocks accepted their position among the alpha stocks, they co-opted allegorical metaphors to create religious doctrines that would be used to assert the alpha position nature did not default to them.

This goes deeper because the doctrines also set the ideology that relegated women to positions of silence, submission under the rule of men, objects of lust (women must cover up but men don't have to control their urges) and procreation, and servants of all male deities. It is rather ironic how women are created in the images of men within Abrahamic religions; there are no women in the divinity. Where there was once a triune of father, mother and child, the triune of father, son and holy ghost emerged. This is when bitches ain't shit became a reality and how this all ties back into toxic femininity.

The idea that bitches ain't shit puts us against women in all regards. By now we understand the plethora of factors that cause us to operate through the lens of toxic femininity as Black men. We have also observed the foundation to which this operation was built on and accepted. Once we operate through this polarity, we shift the harmony of masculine and feminine to the opposition of femininities. Rather than using our intelligence to balance with a woman's intuition, we use insecurity to battle intuition. Rather than using rationale to balance with emotionality, we use irrationality to battle emotionality. Basically, rather than using masculinity to balance with femininity, we use toxic femininity to battle femininity. This battle is manifested in real time as the essences of masculinity and femininity are expressed by the wielders of the predisposition.

When Black men accept the doctrines which once enslaved them, we engage in toxic femininity. When operating through toxic femininity, we are engaging our sisters with a destructive energy that is combating a constructive energy; leading to a neutralization. This neutralization is the outcome of bitches ain't shit (by now, you gather the allegory in this). Bitches ain't shit evolved from being directed toward our sisters to our people. If the woman ain't shit, neither is the womb. If the womb ain't shit, neither is what emerges. When this outlook becomes a way of life, the value of the people declines. When this way of life is internalized, self-worth also declines as the unconscious mind accepts the stereotype and associates it with the wombs we are birthed from. As self-worth and value for the people decline, the

coon-dilini begins to rise; and self-hatred is
the manifestation. Damn, (why) bitches ain't
shit.

COON-DILINI

A coon has many definitions and expressions within our culture; ranging from sellout to pacifier. For the context of this writing, a coon is defined as one who denies the reality of the collective through the compromise of their personal identity for the acceptance and assimilation into systems of oppression. Coons aren't gender specific; nor are they limited to age or intellect. Furthermore, all coons do not side with their oppositions. Many are against opposition and self in a delusional plot twist. In whichever facet, they are the greatest manifestation of toxic femininity that can emerge from our people; and Black men in regards to this writing. When the coon-dilini rises, cultural destruction of some sort is soon to follow.

Let me first explain that cooning isn't exclusive to buck dancing, foot shuffling and head scratching. Let me make that clear and understood. Although those are the most readily identifiable methods, they are far from being the only forms. Cooning has layers to it. The deeper, more covert the layer, the more damage it does to our people. Cooning includes being a real nigga, a kumbaya passivist and a religious zealot. These are the highest forms of cooning. They are responsible for self-destruction and/or an appeal for morality from immoral beings. In some fashion, these positions destroy the being physically (real nigga), mentally (kumbaya passivist) and spiritually (religious zealot); all results of toxic femininity's manifestation in the absence of masculinity.

When it comes to real niggas, real niggas are only real among niggas. (I view my brothers as brothers but I am using niggas for dramatic effect). The typical real nigga is a gangster, drug dealer, rapper or a persona rooted within one of these; typically. The average real nigga keeps a gun (glock, draco, chopper, etc.) to bang on, ride on, ride for or against...niggas. Their "respect" is a matter of invoking fear and terror within niggas (little, bitch, fake, etc.). They keep this position alive through tyranny among niggas to become the realest nigga. Yet, it seems that real niggas become timid when niggas aren't involved. Real niggas can lose one of their niggas to niggas and go get those niggas that night. Masked up, clips loaded; massacre the entire block. Real nigga shit. Yet, if real niggas lose one of their niggas to a racist cop or vigilante, niggas suddenly run out of guns, ammo and alibis. It's mind blowing really. Real coon shit if you ask me. Now, don't get me wrong. I'm not saying in any way, shape, form or fashion to kill your enemy as you would easily kill

your brother. I'm just asking, "Why not?"
Maybe real niggas don't oppose oppression. I
don't know. I digress. Still coon shit though.

When it comes to kumbaya passivists,
let me explain something to you. It is
irrational to appeal to the morality of beings
who continuously prove to be immoral by
nature. It should not take 500 years of horrific
conditions to come to terms with the idea that
this is a war. It is stupid to follow the
ideology and moral philosophy given to you
by the very person not following them. You
be the bigger person while they continue to be
the smaller person. We say "hands up, don't
shoot," their response is "arms up, blast." We
say "I can't breathe," they respond with "I can
breathe." We say "Justice, or else," they say,
"Or else, what?" We say "Black lives matter,"
they say "Haha, yea right." When we show up
as kumbaya passivists, my brothers, we are
accepting and projecting a reality that what
occurs is okay. Granted, I know they say

violence begets more violence. However, history, their history, shows that enough violence leads to a peace treaty. It's coonish to become a passivist in the wake of active assaults. Again, I am not saying engage in a manner that will force you to brutally murder and correct those who are brutally murdering you. I'm asking, "Why not?" Maybe the kumbaya passivists oppose only the oppression and not the oppressor. I don't know. I digress. Still coon shit though.

Of all the coon-dilini risings, I feel that the risings within the religious zealot are the worst. I am not demeaning or degrading religious beliefs. However, if your religious beliefs support and strengthen your oppression and oppressor, it's time to thoroughly analyze and deconstruct those philosophies. Viewed objectively, it is of complete insanity to knowingly accept that your beliefs came from your oppressor, that your oppressor has lied about and manipulated everything given to you and this very oppressor has done everything to erase your existence, only to accept that what was provided to appeal to your soul is of benefit to you and your people. Yet, here we are.

We operate under a system that simultaneously teaches to love slave masters and give enemies another cheek to slap while encouraging the abuse of offspring through a rod of correction. Objectively, this makes no sense. My children, extensions of myself who are still learning the world, are to be handled physically when they make a mistake. Yet, a defined enemy, who is a coherent adult as myself, is to receive a pass and an opportunity to repeat the wrong a second time. Moreover, it is encouraged that I pray for and forgive them because they know not what they do. It would logically make more sense that this idea should be applied to my children and the rod to my enemy. How can my enemies receive more leniency than the mini beings I created? Also, when the oppressed and the oppressor pray to the same deity, whose prayers are answered? I mean, I'm not saying beat your enemy and give your children a second chance. I'm asking, "Why not?" Maybe religious zealots are serving their purpose in their oppression. I don't know. I digress. Still coon shit though. In the grand scheme of it all, this coon shit may be the coon shit that makes the other coon shit possible. All euphemistically speaking, of course. But I digress.

Historically speaking, a real nigga, a good slave and devout believer are the same thing. No oppressed people have ever left their oppression without the behaviors of their oppressors. Their mentality and spirituality is grounded by the roots that ground the beings that oppose them. This is a pivotal piece that allows toxic femininity to infuse into their divinity. We understand that femininity is the physical, mental and spiritual embodiment of

132

the essence of synthesis and construction. When this embodiment is made toxic, destruction and destructive practices are the only manifestations that will be expressed and exhibited. As men, if my brothers and I create a world through this polarity, we horribly disservice ourselves, our families, our communities and our people. When the coon-dilini rises, we all become willing participants in our own demise. Stop cooning my brothers. Not only our survival, but our existence depends on it.

FINAL WORDS

Femininity is an important piece in our existence as beings. It is the point that makes us manifesting creators. Without our feminine component, the most we can be in our highest masculine capacity are vessels who can deconstruct and analyze our environments. This leads to our natural divinity being half expressed. In its healthiest capacity our feminine nature allows us to create in the most dynamic manner. The masculine polarity analyzes and deconstructs our reality and our feminine polarity synthesizes and constructs the raw materials into new creations. In the most toxic capacity, our feminine nature causes us to destroy with

the raw materials obtained by our masculinity.
When we operate through this lens, we are of
no benefit to ourselves, our families or our
people.

The toxic femininity that we have
adopted through oppression, integration and
assimilation into an insane societal structure
has taken over our entire being. Our
physicality, mentality and spirituality are in
the twilight zone, so to speak. The deeper we
slip into this structure, the more we destroy
ourselves. I respect all that the Civil Rights
movement attempted to do. I do not bash or
despise the leaders. However, the movement
did not work. We must acknowledge this. It is
broken and does not work for us. Even Dr.
King was quoted saying, "I fear I may have
integrated my people into a burning house."
I'm simply expressing that the house is,
indeed, on fire; and I refuse to allow us to
continue saying, "It's just a little warm in

here, we'll adjust." That's completely ridiculous and stupid.

Since integrating into this structure we've lost businesses, schools, land, our damned minds, you name it. All in the name of "equality and love." It is this moment that I observed that masculinity is obsolete. Intelligence and rationale were found nowhere in this bright idea. The premise of appealing to the morality of immoral people by infusing into their space in one of their more volatile points of history was not logical. Yet, we did just that. Not only did we do that, we did it passively under the guise that "the world will see that they are wrong and they will eventually see the error in their ways." Fast forward 50+ years and they have not learned the error of their ways. Rather they taught these ways to their children; who taught them to their children. And we taught it to our children; who taught it to their children. Why? Because we operated through emotion and subjective expressions (femininity) that matched an idea that "One day, there would be a world where…" Yes, there may come a day when that is a reality. However, that day is not today, tomorrow or next week. This is the outcome of operating through femininity in an era of tragedy.

By operating through femininity and infusing into a poisonous societal structure, toxic femininity was inevitable. Nothing constructive emerges from a toxic feminine society. Whatsoever. War, poverty, oppression, misogyny, rape, castration, genocide; these are all manifestations of toxic femininity. A world governed by toxic feminine, pheomelaninated men is what we desired to assimilate to. Now we exhibit their behaviors within our eumelaninated minds and souls. We think with the minds of the beings we integrated with. We view and treat our women as they do. We murder our own brothers as they would. We are in a fornication of the mind that is allowing us be passivists, coons and real niggas who are injecting the toxins they've created to kill us, for them.

As with the first installment of So Frail, this is not a means to degrade, demean or demoralize my brothers. We are great. However, we cannot reach our pinnacle until we address the toxic femininity. Accept its imposition on us and revive our healthy expressions in harmony with our masculinity. The time for this is now. We were already too late when Martin's legacy eclipsed Malcolm's in the mainstream. We became completely off when Al and Jesse became favored over Huey and Bobby. At this moment, not another generation can continue this way. WE must stop this. Now.

I hope that my words and observations have sparked something within your mind. We are in a heavy battle right now where we are attacked on deeper levels. This attack is led by the continuous reaffirming of toxic femininity within our beings. It makes us destructive to ourselves, our people and our communities. It's beyond "unplugging from the matrix." If the mentality is not adjusted, the manifestation will always occur; no matter what. I don't have all of the solutions and I don't claim to. However, something has to be done and imprinted for the future generations. We may not see it come to fruition but we can at least be a piece to get the ball rolling. I was sparked so I will spark without the worries of what may happen to me. As 'Pac said, "...I'm not saying I'm gonna rule the world or I'm gonna change the world, but I guarantee that I will spark the brain that will change the world." Here's my spark.

~PEACE, LOVE, KNOWLEDGE AND
FREEDOM~